on Literacy

Starter Level
Skills Pack

Karina Law

Collins

Published by Collins
A division of HarperCollins*Publishers* Ltd
77–85 Fulham Palace Road
Hammersmith
London W6 8JB

www.**Collins**Education.com
On-line Support for Schools and Colleges

www.**fireandwater**.com
Visit the book lover's website

First published 2001

© HarperCollins*Publishers* Ltd 2001

10 9 8 7 6 5

All rights reserved. Any educational institution that has purchased one copy of this book may make duplicate copies of pages identified as copiable for use exclusively within that institution. (Copiable pages can be identified by the copyright notice printed at the bottom of the page.) Permission does not extend to reproduction, storage in a retrieval system, or transmission in any form or by any means – electronic, mechanical, photocopying, recording or otherwise – of duplicate copies for lending, renting or selling to any other user or institution without the prior consent, in writing, of the publisher.

ISBN 0 00 711098 7

Karina Law asserts the moral right to be identified as the author of this work.

Series editors: Barry and Anita Scholes
Design: Perry Tate Design
Editor: Sue Chapple
Illustrator: Juliet Breese
Cover design: Grasshopper Design Company
Cover image: Gary Hunter/Tony Stone Images
Scottish Curriculum referencing: Eleanor McMillan

Acknowledgements
The author and publishers would like to thank:
Pat O'Brien and all at English Martyrs RC Primary School, Liverpool.

Printed in Great Britain by Martins the Printers, Berwick-upon-Tweed

Contents

Skills Masters: Term 1 1 – 40

Skills Masters: Term 2 41 – 80

Skills Masters: Term 3 81 – 120

Skills Masters for general use

High frequency words 1 121

High frequency words 2 122

High frequency words 3 123

Word wheel 124

Word slide 125

Skills Master Unit 1

Name

Pp is for princess

Write the letter **p**.

p p p p p _ _ _ _ _

Circle the things that begin with **p**.

Focus on Literacy Starter Level Skills Pack © HarperCollinsPublishers Ltd 2001

Skills Master 2 Unit 1

Name _____

Invitation

Finish the invitation.

To _____

Please come for _____

at _____

on _____

Love from _____

x x x

Focus on Literacy Starter Level Skills Pack © HarperCollinsPublishers Ltd 2001

Love from

Thank you for

To

Thank you!

UNIT 1 SKILLS MASTER 3
Focus on Literacy Starter Level Skills Pack
© HarperCollins*Publishers* Ltd 2001

Skills Master 4
Unit 1

Name _____

Bb is for beastie

Write the letter **b**.

b b b b b b _ _ _ _ _

Draw the foods that begin with **b** in this beastie's tummy.

Focus on Literacy Starter Level Skills Pack © HarperCollinsPublishers Ltd 2001

Name _____

Good days and bad days

In our class we have ...

good days

bad days

Skills Master **5**
Unit **2**

Focus on Literacy Starter Level Skills Pack © HarperCollins*Publishers* Ltd 2001

Skills Master 6
Unit 2

Name _____

The best day ever

What would you do?

In the morning I would...

In the afternoon I would...

Focus on Literacy Starter Level Skills Pack © HarperCollins*Publishers* Ltd 2001

Skills Master 7　Unit 2

Name _____

Happy or sad?

Join each picture to the correct word.

sad　　happy

What things make you happy or sad?

Skills Master 8
Unit 2

Name _____

How do they feel?

Write the correct word in each space.

happy   sad   angry

He feels _____.

They feel _____.

She feels _____.

Focus on Literacy Starter Level Skills Pack © HarperCollins*Publishers* Ltd 2001

**Skills Master 9
Unit 3**

Name _____

Swimming

Match the correct words to each picture.

| This is fun. | We're going swimming. |
| Jump in! | Get undressed. |

Skills Master 10
Unit 3

Name _____

Words with u

Write the letter.

| m s b |

___un

___ug

___us

Write four more -ug words.

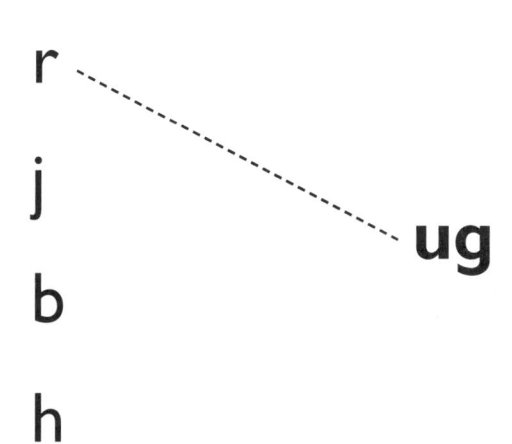

r
j   ug
b
h

rug
____
____
____

Skills Master 11 Unit 3

Name _____

What are they saying?

Write the words that each person is saying.

Skills Master 12 Unit 3

Name _____

Let's go swimming

Circle the things you need for swimming.

Focus on Literacy Starter Level Skills Pack © HarperCollinsPublishers Ltd 2001

Skills Master 13
Unit 4

Name _____

The Seven Dwarfs

This house belongs to the Seven Dwarfs.

1. Colour the door red.
2. Colour the roses pink.
3. Colour the roof yellow.

How many windows can you see?

I can see _____ windows.

Skills Master 14
Unit 4

Name _____

Whose house?

Find the matching pictures.

| bed | lamp | jug | pan |

| chair | rug | sink | mop |

Focus on Literacy Starter Level Skills Pack © HarperCollins*Publishers* Ltd 2001

Skills Master 15
Unit 4

Name

Goldilocks

Put the pictures in the right order. Tell the story.

Skills Master 16
Unit 4

Name

A letter

Finish the letter.

Goldileaf Cottage
Leafy Lane
The Woods

Dear Bears,

I am very sorry that I _____

_____

_____

_____

Love from

Goldilocks

Focus on Literacy Starter Level Skills Pack © HarperCollinsPublishers Ltd 2001

Skills Master 17 Unit 5

Name _____

What can they do?

Write the correct word in each space.

> hop   skip   run   swim

He can _____.   She can _____.

She can _____.   They can _____.

Focus on Literacy Starter Level Skills Pack © HarperCollins*Publishers* Ltd 2001

Skills Master 18
Unit **5**

Name _____

I can ...

Finish the sentences.

I can _____.

I can _____.

**Skills Master 19
Unit 5**

Name _____

I wish ...

What do you wish?

I wish _____

_____

_____.

Skills Master 20 Unit 5

Name _____

Who can do it?

Write the correct word in each space.

> he   she   they

_____ can skip   _____ can read

_____ can swim   _____ can jump

Focus on Literacy Starter Level Skills Pack © HarperCollinsPublishers Ltd 2001

Skills Master 21
Unit 6

Name _____

Which letter?

Say the name. Write the first letter.   f   n   p   t

Focus on Literacy Starter Level Skills Pack © HarperCollins*Publishers* Ltd 2001

Noses, feet and tails

Join each nose, foot and tail to the correct animal.

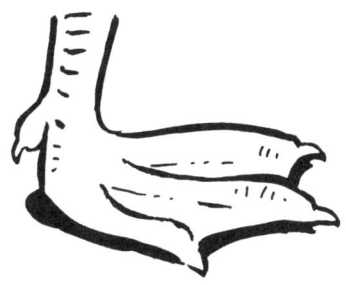

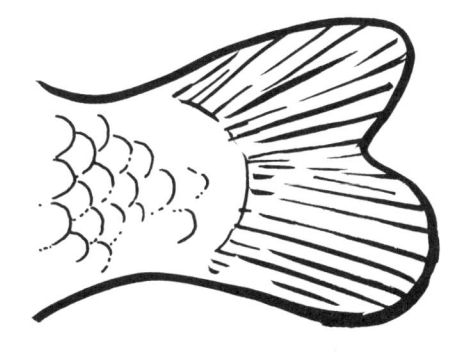

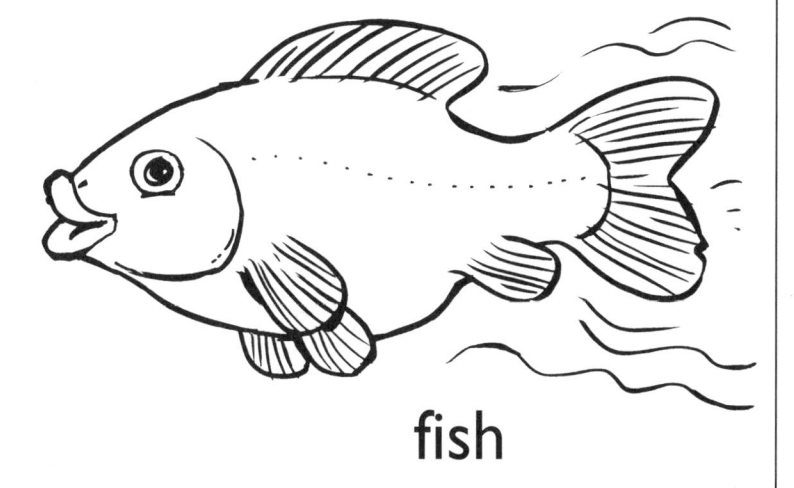

dog

duck

fish

**Skills Master 23
Unit 6**

Name _____

I spy

I spy with my little eye…

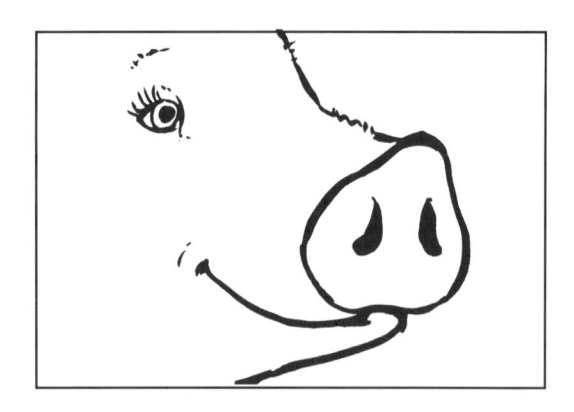

…something beginning with ____.

…something beginning with ____.

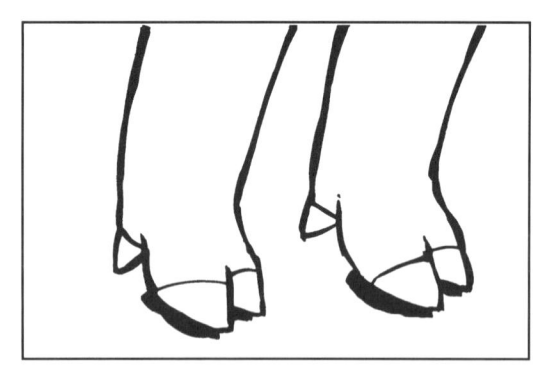

…something beginning with ____.

What am I?

I am a _____.

Skills Master 24
Unit 6

Name _____

Label the dog

Cut out the words. Stick them in the correct places.

nose   paw   tail

ear   claw

Focus on Literacy Starter Level Skills Pack © HarperCollinsPublishers Ltd 2001

Skills Master 25
Unit 7

Name _____

How many?

Count the things in each picture. Write the correct number word in the space.

| 1 one | 2 two | 3 three |
| 4 four | 5 five | 6 six |

_____ bus

_____ dogs

_____ pigs

_____ bats

_____ cats

_____ rats

Focus on Literacy Starter Level Skills Pack © HarperCollinsPublishers Ltd 2001

Skills Master 26
Unit 7

Name _____

If you're happy

Write the correct words under each picture.

Clap your hands.
Stamp your feet.

Nod your head.
Wave your hands.

_____
_____

_____
_____

_____
_____

_____
_____

Focus on Literacy Starter Level Skills Pack © HarperCollins*Publishers* Ltd 2001

Skills Master 27
Unit 7

Name _____

My hands

Write each word in the correct space.

wash   eat   clap   wave

I can _____ my hands.

I can _____ my hands.

I can _____ my hands.

I can _____ with my hands.

Focus on Literacy Starter Level Skills Pack © HarperCollins*Publishers* Ltd 2001

Skills Master 28
Unit 7

Name _____

Finger puppets

1. Colour the two birds.

2. Carefully cut out each bird along the dotted lines.

3. Ask an adult to help you cut out the finger holes. Try on your finger puppets!

Focus on Literacy Starter Level Skills Pack © HarperCollins*Publishers* Ltd 2001

Skills Master 29
Unit 8

Name _____

Ww is for weather

Write the letter **w**.

w w w w w w ___ ___ ___

Write **w** in the box next to things that begin with **w**.

Focus on Literacy Starter Level Skills Pack © HarperCollins*Publishers* Ltd 2001

Skills Master 30
Unit 8

Name _____

Sun

Look at the letters in the rain drops.

Write four **-un** words.

sun

s

b

r

f

Answer **yes** or **no**.

Is the sun near? _____

Is the sun a star? _____

Is the sun hot? _____

Focus on Literacy Starter Level Skills Pack © Harper*Collins*Publishers Ltd 2001

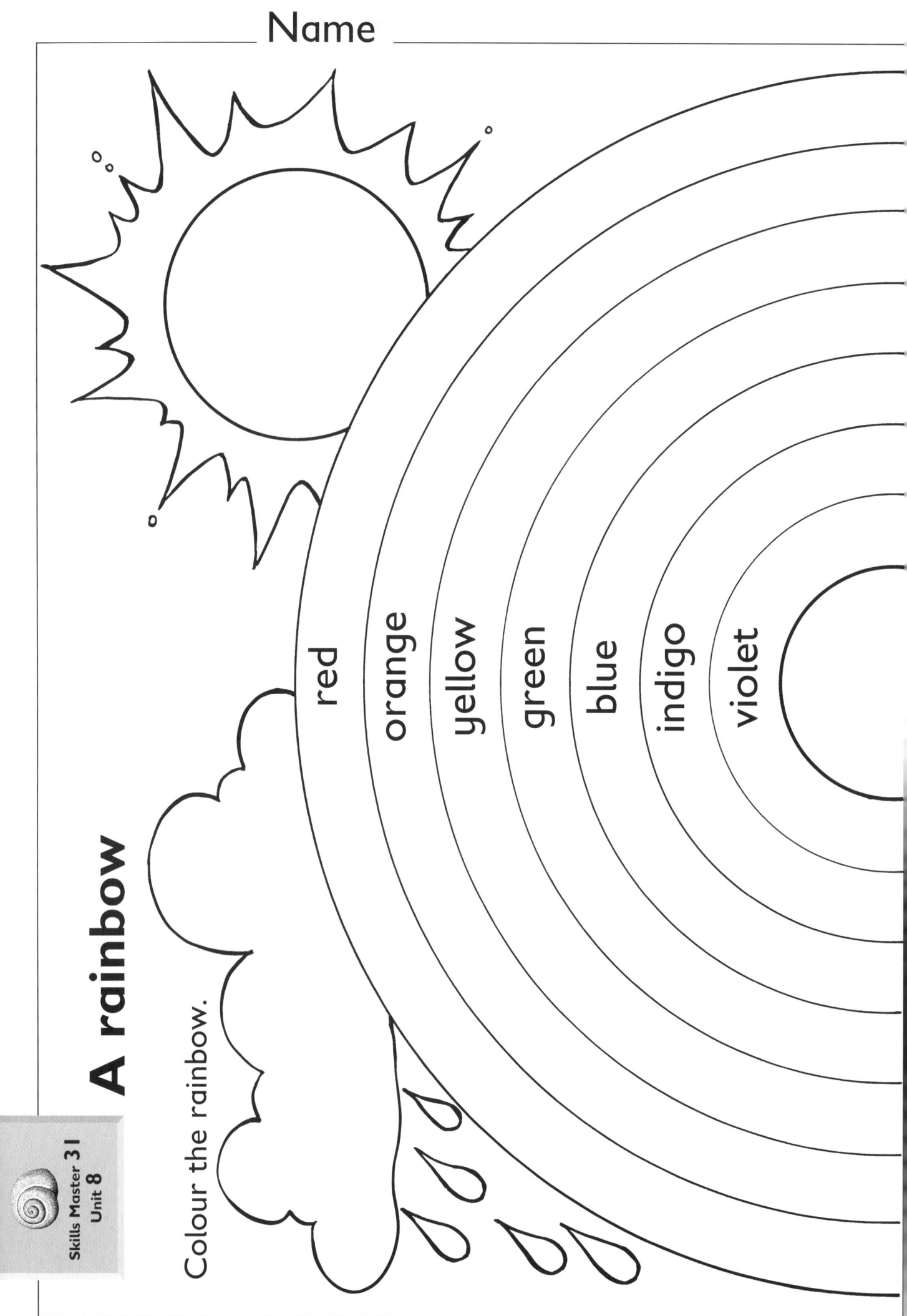

Name _____

A rainbow

Colour the rainbow.

- red
- orange
- yellow
- green
- blue
- indigo
- violet

Skills Master 31
Unit 8

Skills Master 32
Unit 8

Name _____

Weather chart

This month is _____.

	What is the weather like?
Monday	
Tuesday	
Wednesday	
Thursday	
Friday	

sunny foggy rainy windy

cold cloudy stormy frosty

Focus on Literacy Starter Level Skills Pack © HarperCollins*Publishers* Ltd 2001

Skills Master 33
Unit 9

Name _____

New toys

Write the first letter of each word.

b c d j p t

__oll   __ar   __eddy

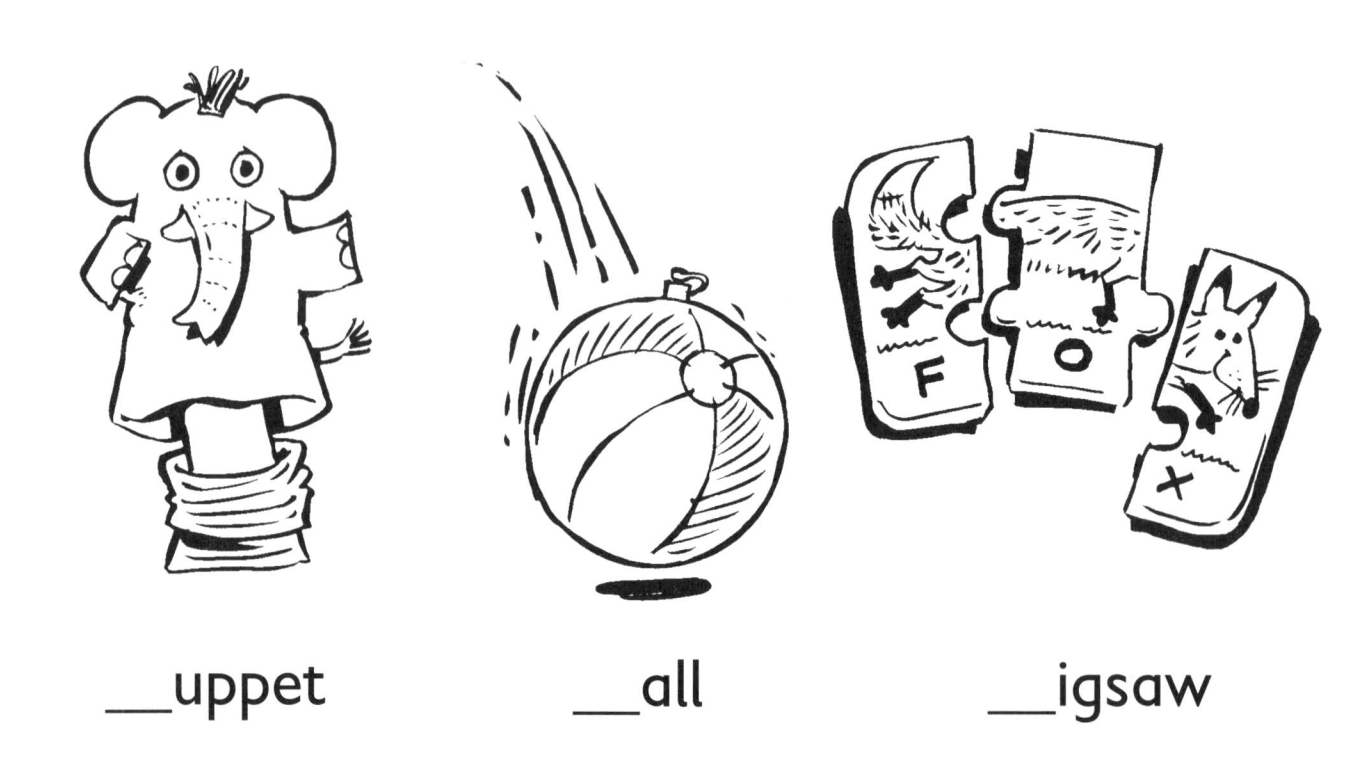

__uppet   __all   __igsaw

Skills Master 34
Unit 9

Name _____

My best toy

Draw a picture of your best toy here.

This is my best toy. It is a _____.

I like this toy best because _____

_____.

Focus on Literacy Starter Level Skills Pack © HarperCollins*Publishers* Ltd 2001

Skills Master 35
Unit 9

Name _____

Tt is for toys

Write the letter **t**.

t   t   t   t   t   ___ ___ ___

Write **t** in the box next to things that begin with **t**.

Focus on Literacy Starter Level Skills Pack © HarperCollinsPublishers Ltd 2001

Skills Master 36 Unit 9

Name _____

In the toy shop

Find these toys in the shop window.
Draw a line from each word to the matching picture.

- yo-yo
- teddy
- doll
- kite
- jigsaw
- ball
- ship

Which toy would you choose?

I would choose the _____.

Focus on Literacy Starter Level Skills Pack © HarperCollins*Publishers* Ltd 2001

Skills Master 37
Unit 10

Name _____

Kk is for kitten

✏️ Write the letter **k**.

k k k k k k ___ ___ ___ ___

Write **k** in the box next to things that begin with **k**.

Focus on Literacy Starter Level Skills Pack © HarperCollins*Publishers* Ltd 2001

**Skills Master 38
Unit 10**

Name _____

Cc is for cat

Write the letter **c**.

c c c c c c __ __ __ __ __

Write **c** in the box next to things that begin with **c**.

Focus on Literacy Starter Level Skills Pack © HarperCollinsPublishers Ltd 2001

Skills Master 39
Unit 10

Name _____

Cats and rats

Write words that rhyme with **cat**.

b
f
h
m
p
r
s

cat

Skills Master 40
Unit 10

Name _____

Christmas presents

Choose presents for your friends. Write the labels.

To _____
From _____

To _____
From _____

To _____
From _____

To _____
From _____

Focus on Literacy Starter Level Skills Pack © HarperCollinsPublishers Ltd 2001

**Skills Master 41
Unit 11**

Name _____

Grandpa's teds

Help grandpa get the teds ready for bed.
Put the pictures in the right order. Tell the story.

Skills Master 42
Unit 11

Name _____

Hh is for Humpty

Write the letter **h**.

h h h h h h __ __ __ __ __

Read the words on Humpty's wall.

hot   hen   cat

big   he   hop

sit   hat   me   him

Colour the bricks with words that begin with **h**.

Focus on Literacy Starter Level Skills Pack © HarperCollinsPublishers Ltd 2001

Name

Humpty and Hugh

Skills Master 43
Unit 11

Tell the story.

1	2
_____	_____
_____	_____

3	4
_____	_____
_____	_____

Skills Master 44
Unit 11

Name _____

Rhyming fun

Join the pictures that rhyme.

Skills Master 45
Unit 12

Name _____

Gg is for grandad

Write the letter **g**.

g g g g g g ___ ___ ___ ___

Write **g** in the box next to things that begin with **g**.

Focus on Literacy Starter Level Skills Pack © HarperCollins*Publishers* Ltd 2001

Skills Master 46
Unit 12

Name _____

Grandad's garden

Circle all the things that begin with **g**.

How many things did you find that begin with **g**?

I found _____ things.

Skills Master 47
Unit 12

Name _____

A letter to Grandad

Finish the letter.

Police Station
999 Letsbe Avenue
Dunstable

Dear Grandad,

You must stop _____

_____

_____

_____

Signed
P.C. Law

Skills Master 48
Unit 12

Name _____

Grandad's plant

Put the pictures in the right order. Tell the story.

_____
_____

_____
_____

_____
_____

_____
_____

Skills Master 49
Unit 13

Name _____

Words beginning with t

Write the letter **t** in each space.

__ap

__ip

__op

__en

__in

__ug

Read the words you have made.

Skills Master 50
Unit 13

Name _____

The farmer's pets

The farmer's pets are hiding. Can you help him find them?
Write the correct word in each space.

cat   dog   in

The mouse is _____ a cup.

The _____ is up a tree.

The _____ is under the table.

Focus on Literacy Starter Level Skills Pack © HarperCollins*Publishers* Ltd 2001

Skills Master 51
Unit 13

Name _____

The Enormous Turnip

Tell the story.

1	2
3	4

_____   _____

_____   _____

_____   _____

_____   _____

Focus on Literacy Starter Level Skills Pack © HarperCollins*Publishers* Ltd 2001

Skills Master 52
Unit 13

Name _____

Down on the farm

Circle all the things that begin with **t**.

How many things did you find that begin with **t**?

I found _____ things.

Focus on Literacy Starter Level Skills Pack © HarperCollinsPublishers Ltd 2001

Name _____

What shall we do today?

Skills Master 53
Unit 14

Join each picture to the correct sentence.

Read a book.

Build up bricks.

Draw and paint.

What else will you do?

_____
_____

**Skills Master 54
Unit 14**

Name _____

Wet play

Wet play! Wet play!
What are we going to do today?

_____

_____

That's what I shall do!

Skills Master 55
Unit 14

Name _____

Lost property

What have the children lost?
Read the sentences.
Find the lost things and circle them.

I've lost my bag.

I've lost my hat.

I've lost my ted.

Focus on Literacy Starter Level Skills Pack © HarperCollins*Publishers* Ltd 2001

This book belongs to me

This book belongs to

This book belongs to

Skills Master 56
Unit 14

Focus on Literacy Starter Level Skills Pack © HarperCollins*Publishers* Ltd 2001

Skills Master 57
Unit 15

Name _____

Jj is for jungle

Write the letter **j**.

j j j j j j ___ ___ ___ ___ ___

Write **j** in the box next to things that begin with **j**.

**Skills Master 58
Unit 15**

Name _____

Deep in the jungle

Deep in the jungle

where the tall trees grow

see the _____.

Mind how you go!

Deep in the jungle

where the tall trees grow

see the _____.

Mind how you go!

**Skills Master 59
Unit 15**

Name _____

ch is for chimpanzee

Write **ch** in the box next to things that begin with **ch**.

Focus on Literacy Starter Level Skills Pack © HarperCollinsPublishers Ltd 2001

**Skills Master 60
Unit 15**

Name _____

Colours of the wild

Colour the picture.

y = yellow   **r** = red   **b** = blue
g = green   **p** = purple   **o** = orange

Focus on Literacy Starter Level Skills Pack © HarperCollinsPublishers Ltd 2001

Skills Master 61
Unit 16

Name _____

Rr is for rabbit

Write the letter **r**.

r r r r r r r ___ ___ ___ ___

Circle the things that begin with **r**.

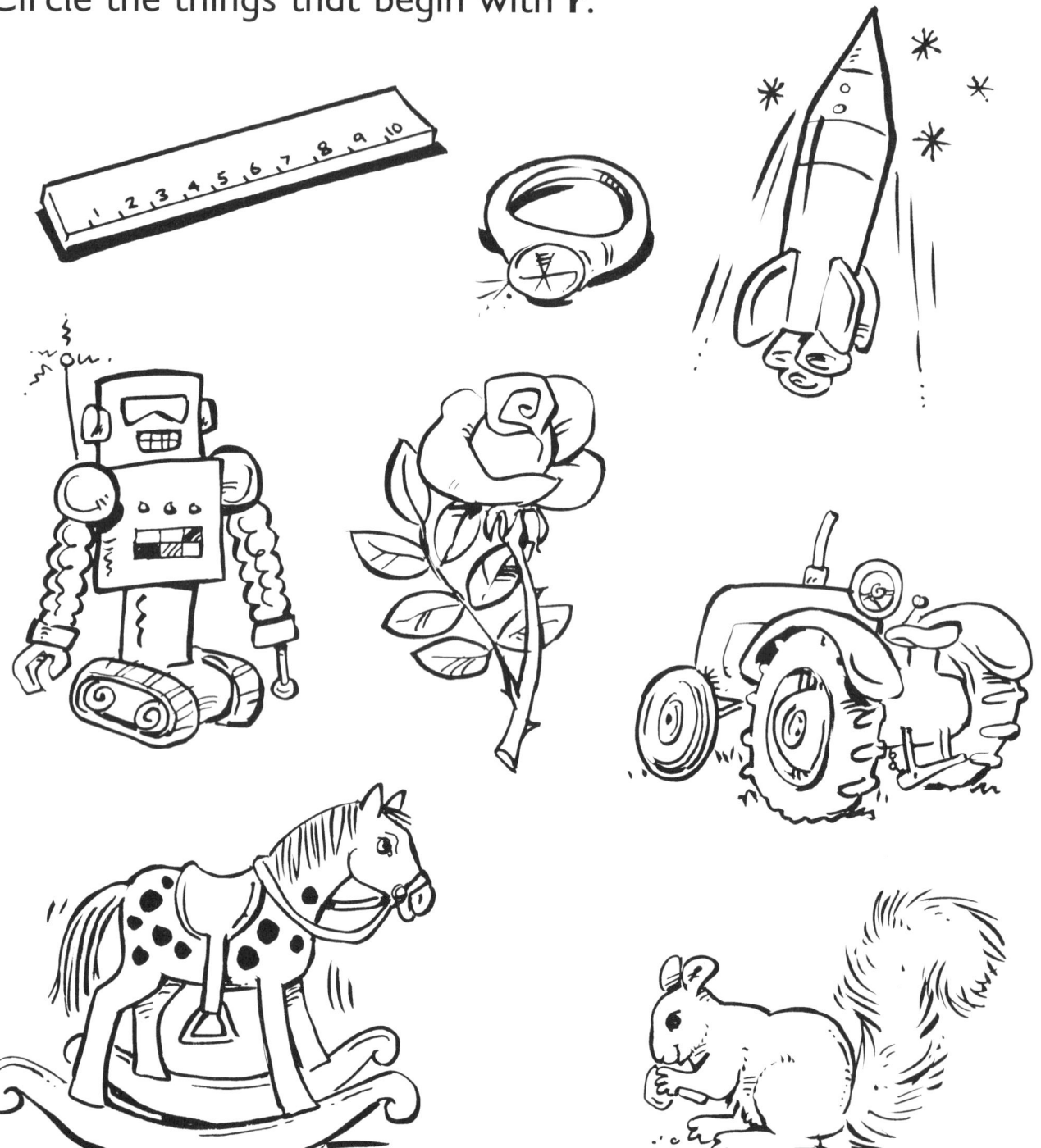

Skills Master 62
Unit 16

Name _____

What do I need?

Put a ✔ next to the things I need.
Put a ✗ next to the things I do not need.

Skills Master 63
Unit 16

Name
Pets and vets

Make words that rhyme with **pet**.

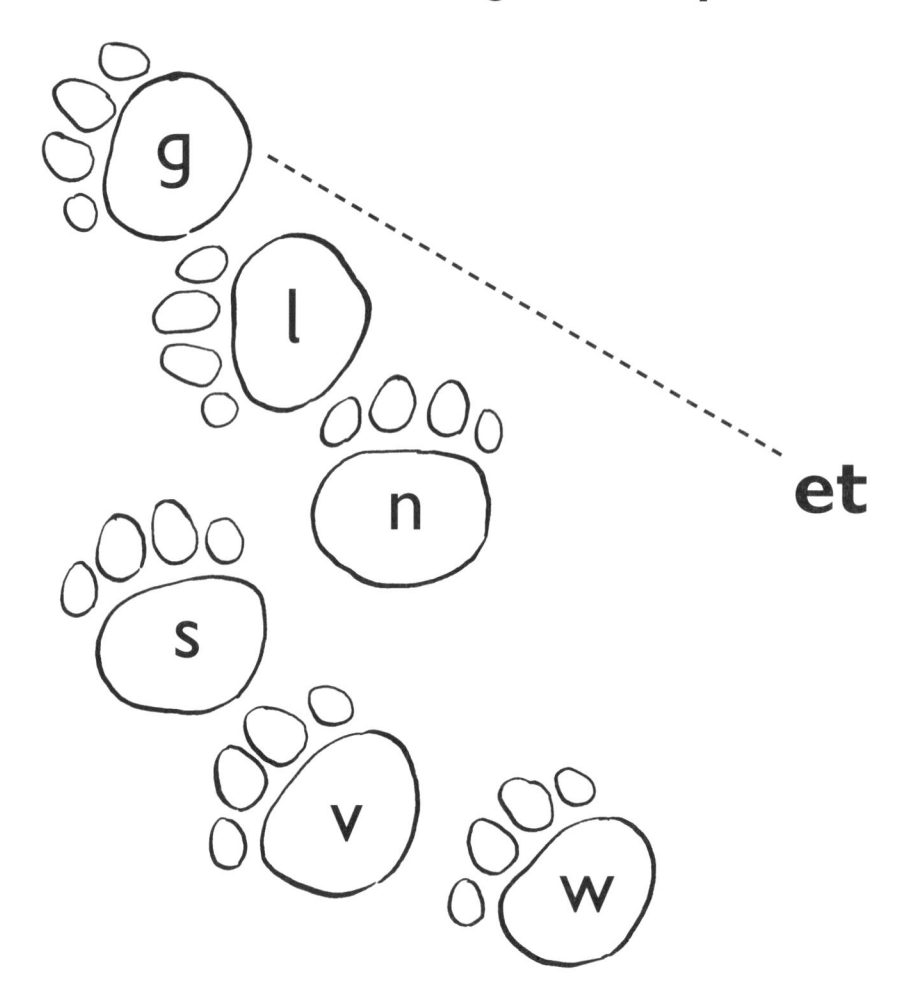

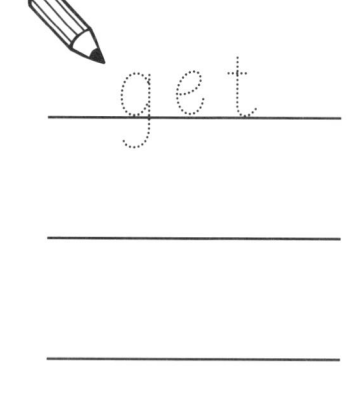

g
l
n
s
v
w

et

get
_____
_____
_____
_____
_____
_____

Write the correct word under each picture.

_____ _____ _____

Skills Master 64
Unit 16

Name _____

Vv is for vet

Write the letter **v**.

v v v v v v

Write **v** in the box next to things that begin with **v**.

Focus on Literacy Starter Level Skills Pack © HarperCollinsPublishers Ltd 2001

Skills Master 65
Unit 17

Name _____

a to z

Join the letters in the right order. What do you see?

a b c d e f g h i j k l m n o p q r s t u v w x y z

**Skills Master 66
Unit 17**

Name _____

Aa is for apple

A a is for ✏️

B b is for

C c is for

D d is for

E e is for

F f is for

G g is for

Focus on Literacy Starter Level Skills Pack © HarperCollins*Publishers* Ltd 2001

Skills Master 67
Unit 17

Name _____

Zz is for zoo

Write the letter **z**.

z z z z z z z _____ _____ _____ _____

Write **z** in the box next to things that begin with **z**.

Skills Master 68 Unit 17

Name _____

Capital letters

Join the letters.

a	A B N	n
b		o
c		p
d	D Q	q
e	E	r
f		s
g	R	t
h	H G	u
i	T	v
j		w
k	I Y	x
l		y
m		z

Focus on Literacy Starter Level Skills Pack © HarperCollins*Publishers* Ltd 2001

Skills Master 69
Unit 18

Name _____

Words with e

Write **e** in each space to make words.

b __ d   h __ n   w __ b

t __ n   n __ t   p __ n

Write each word under the correct picture.

_____   _____   _____

_____   _____   _____

Skills Master 70
Unit 18

Name _____

A broken toy

Tell the story.

1	2
_____	_____
_____	_____

3	4
_____	_____
_____	_____

Focus on Literacy Starter Level Skills Pack © HarperCollins*Publishers* Ltd 2001

Name _____

What is Granny knitting?

Follow Granny's wool to find out what she is knitting.

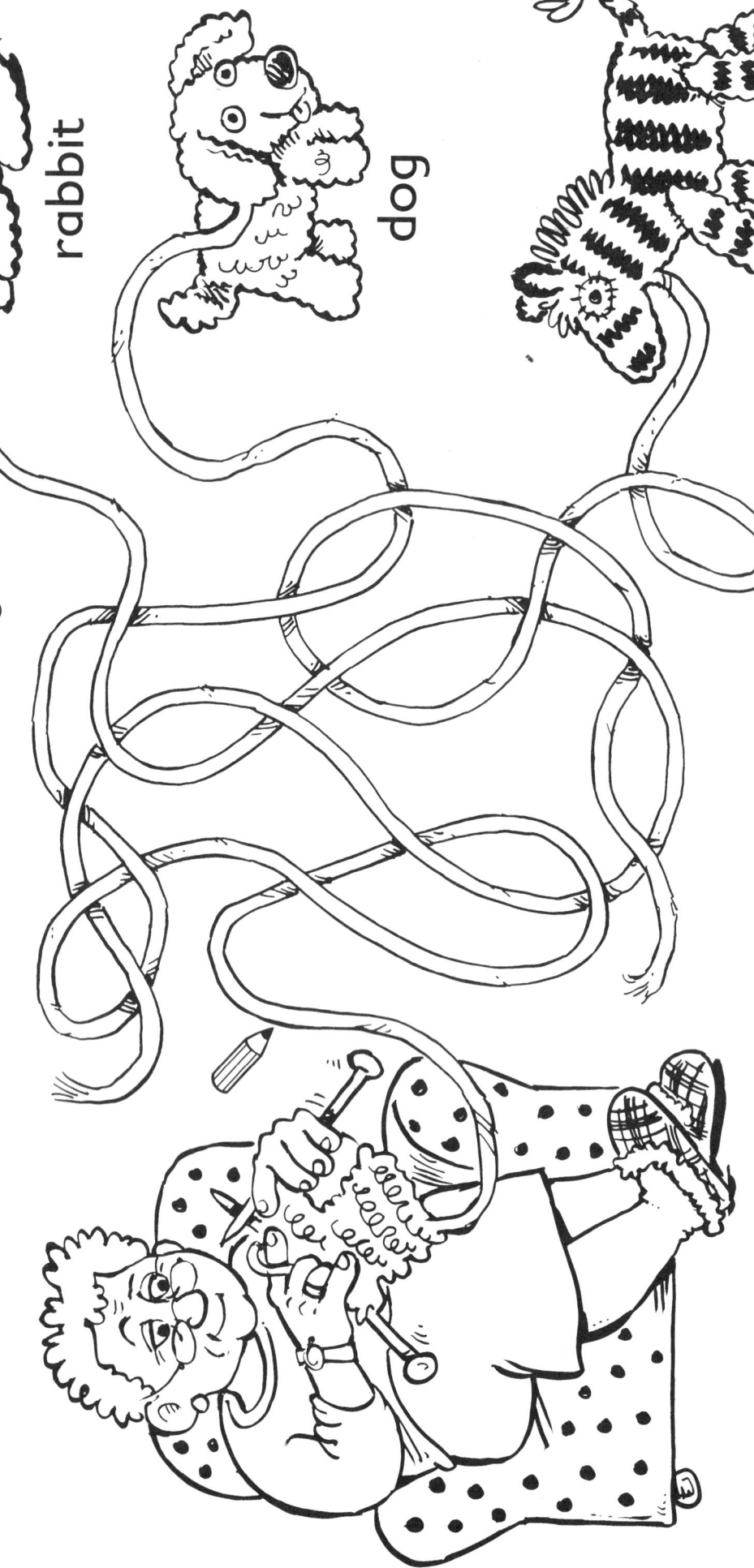

rabbit

dog

zebra

Granny is knitting a _____.

Skills Master 71
Unit 18

Focus on Literacy Starter Level Skills Pack © HarperCollins*Publishers* Ltd 2001

An elephant

Write the missing words.

| fat | no | nose |

An elephant goes like this and that,
He's terribly big,
And he's terribly _____ .
He has no fingers,
And he has _____ toes,
But goodness gracious,
What a long _____ !

Skills Master 73
Unit 19

Name _____

Mary had a little lamb

Write what the teacher is saying.

> Mary had a little lamb
> Its fleece was white as snow,
> And everywhere that Mary went
> The lamb was sure to go.

Skills Master 74
Unit 19

Name _____

Ll is for lion

Write the letter **l**.

l l l l l l _____

Circle the things that begin with **l**.

Focus on Literacy Starter Level Skills Pack © HarperCollins*Publishers* Ltd 2001

Skills Master 75
Unit 19

Name _____

School days

At school we…

Skills Master 76
Unit 19

Name _____

Word chain

Change one letter at a time to make new words.

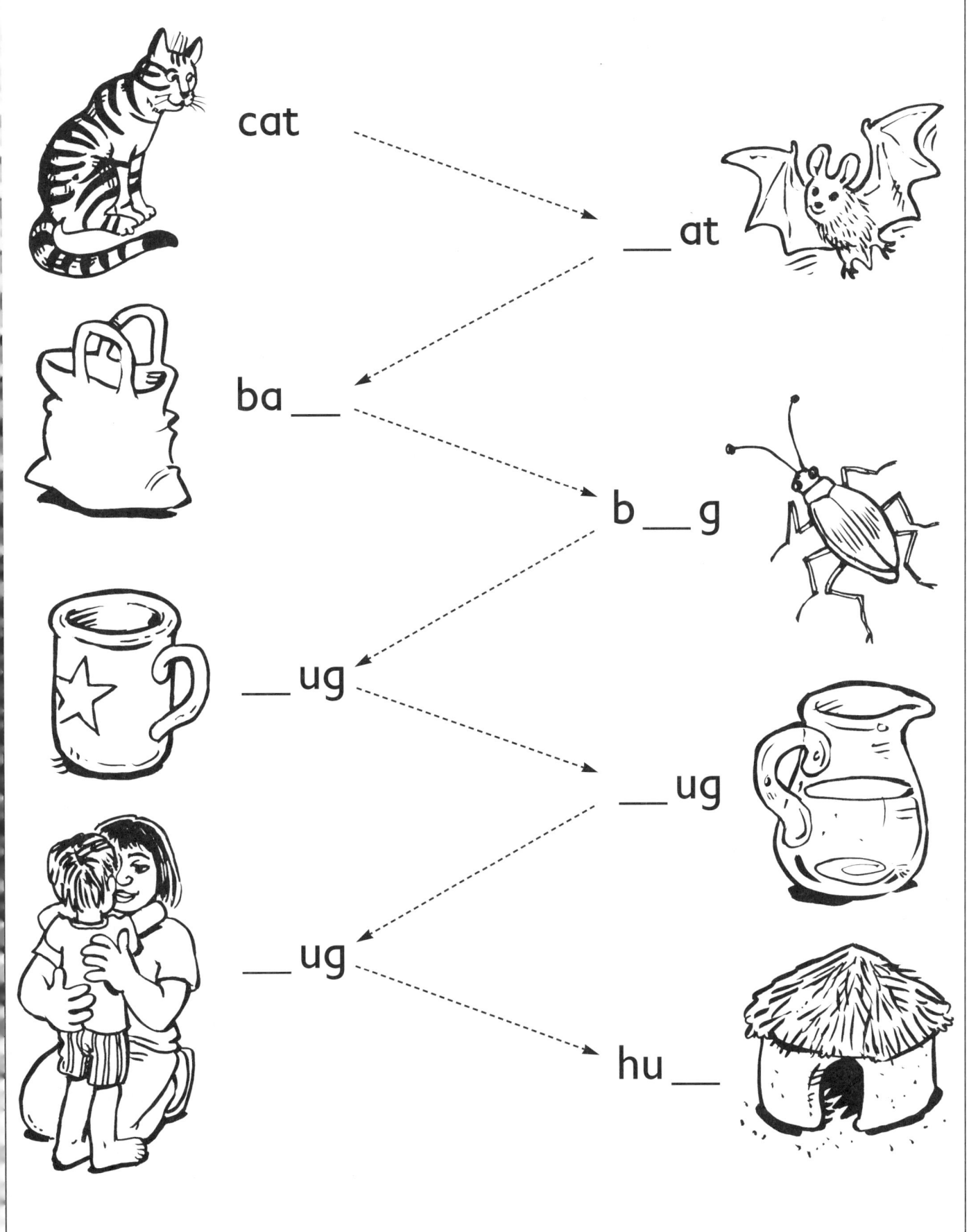

cat

__ at

ba __

b __ g

__ ug

__ ug

__ ug

hu __

Skills Master 77
Unit 20

Name _____

Words with y

Write the letter **y**.

y y y y y y ___ ___ ___ ___

Write **y** in each space to make words.

dr  __   fl  __   cr __

to __ s    fr  __   __ ell

Focus on Literacy Starter Level Skills Pack © HarperCollinsPublishers Ltd 2001

Skills Master 78
Unit 20

Name _____

My favourite season

My favourite season is

_____.

I like it because _____

_____

_____

Focus on Literacy Starter Level Skills Pack © HarperCollins*Publishers* Ltd 2001

Skills Master 79
Unit 20

Name _____

The four seasons

spring	summer
autumn	winter

Cut out the pictures.
Stick them in the seasons where you think they belong.

Add some words and pictures of your own.

Skills Master 80
Unit 20

Name _____

Words beginning with s

Write **s** in each space to make words.

__un   __it   __ad

__et   __ix   __um

Read the words you have made and label the pictures.

_____   _____   _____

Cross out the thing that does not begin with **s**.

Focus on Literacy Starter Level Skills Pack © HarperCollins*Publishers* Ltd 2001

Skills Master 81
Unit 21

Name _____

Words with o

Write the letter **o**.

o o o o o o o ___ ___ ___ ___

Write **o** in each space to make words.

t__p   b__x   p__p

h__p   m__p   f__g

Write the correct word under each picture.

_____   _____   _____

Focus on Literacy Starter Level Skills Pack © HarperCollinsPublishers Ltd 2001

Skills Master 82
Unit 21

Name _____

What is in the box?

Write the missing words.

| mouse | doll | ship | rabbit |

A _____ is in the box.

A _____ is in the box.

A _____ is in the box.

A _____ is in the box.

Focus on Literacy Starter Level Skills Pack © HarperCollinsPublishers Ltd 2001

Skills Master 83
Unit 21

Name _____

Words with x

Write **x** in each space to make words.

bo __   mi __   si __

e __ it   fo __   a __ e

Write the correct word under each picture.

_____   _____   _____

Focus on Literacy Starter Level Skills Pack © HarperCollins*Publishers* Ltd 2001

Name _____

Skills Master 84
Unit 21

A big, big tale

Tell the story.

Once upon a time there was a big, big

Up the   there was a big, big

On the   there was a big, big

At the front of the   there was a big, big

Behind the   there was a big, big

Focus on Literacy Starter Level Skills Pack © HarperCollins*Publishers* Ltd 2001

Skills Master 85
Unit 22

Name _____

People who help us

Join the words to the correct pictures.

dentist

teacher

firefighter

doctor

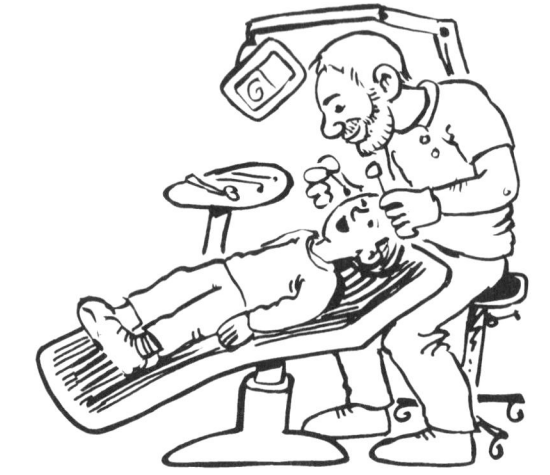

policeman

What number should you call in an emergency? ___ ___ ___

Name _____

A letter for me

Skills Master **86**
Unit **22**

Name _____

Focus on Literacy Starter Level Skills Pack © HarperCollins*Publishers* Ltd 2001

Skills Master 87
Unit 22

Name

Words with th

Write **th** in each space to make words.

__ __e   __ __ree   __ __umb

ba__ __   mo__ __   pa__ __

Write the correct word under each picture.

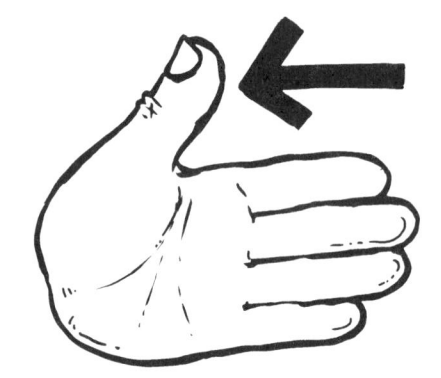

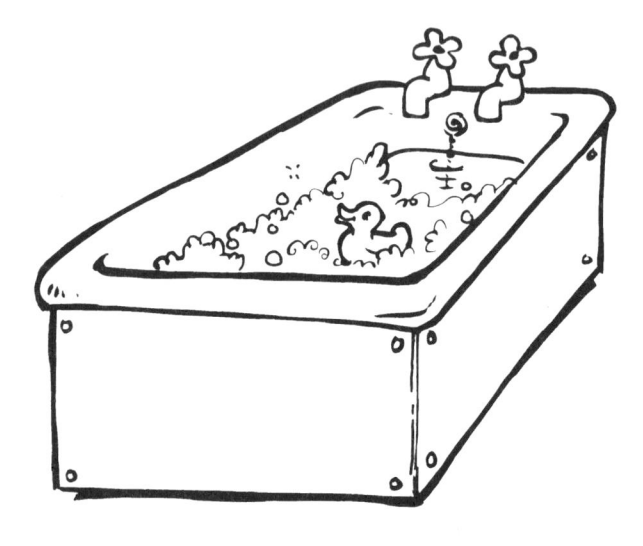

_____   _____   _____

_____   _____

Skills Master 88
Unit 22

Name _____

In the street

Cut out the signs and stick them in the correct places.

QUEEN STREET

BUS 6

FOR SALE

POLICE

BUS STOP

STOP

Focus on Literacy Starter Level Skills Pack © HarperCollins*Publishers* Ltd 2001

Skills Master 89
Unit 23

Name _____

Ss is for sisters

Write the letter **s**.

s s s s s s ___ ___ ___ ___

Circle the things that begin with **s**.

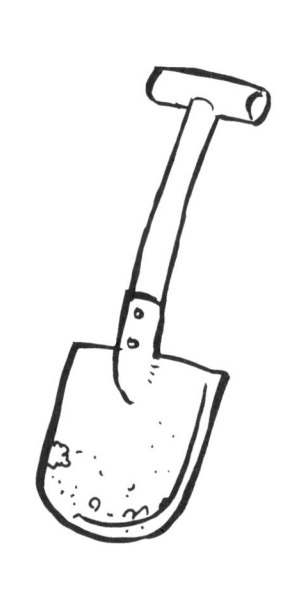

Skills Master 90
Unit 23

Name _____

Menu

Write a menu for a special meal.

Menu

Skills Master 91
Unit 23

Name _____

qu is for queen

The letter **q** is always followed by **u**.

Write the letters **q** and **u**.

qu qu qu ____ ____ ____

____ ____ ____

Write **qu** in each space to make words.

____een   ____ilt   ____iz

____ack   ____estion   ____iet

Write the correct word under each picture.

_____   _____   _____

Focus on Literacy Starter Level Skills Pack © HarperCollinsPublishers Ltd 2001

Skills Master 92
Unit 23

Name _____

Little sister

Write about the picture.

_____
_____
_____

Focus on Literacy Starter Level Skills Pack © HarperCollins*Publishers* Ltd 2001

**Skills Master 93
Unit 24**

Name _____

Dd is for dragon

Write the letter **d**.

d d d d d d ___ ___ ___ ___

Write **d** in the box next to things that begin with **d**.

Skills Master 94
Unit 24

Name _____

Dragons

Cut out the dragons and sort them into alphabetical order.

Can you spell **dragons** with your letters?

Focus on Literacy Starter Level Skills Pack © HarperCollinsPublishers Ltd 2001

Skills Master 95
Unit 24

Name _____

Dragon under the bed

What would you say if you found a dragon under your bed?

What do you think the dragon would say to you?

Skills Master 96
Unit 24

Name _____

Words beginning with d

Write **d** in each space to make words.

__ad   __ay   __og

__ish   __oll   __rum

Join the words to the correct pictures.

drum

duck

dirty

dinosaur

Focus on Literacy Starter Level Skills Pack © HarperCollinsPublishers Ltd 2001

Skills Master 97
Unit 25

Name _____

A big fat hen

Spell the words that rhyme.

big

pig _____

fat

_____ _____

hen

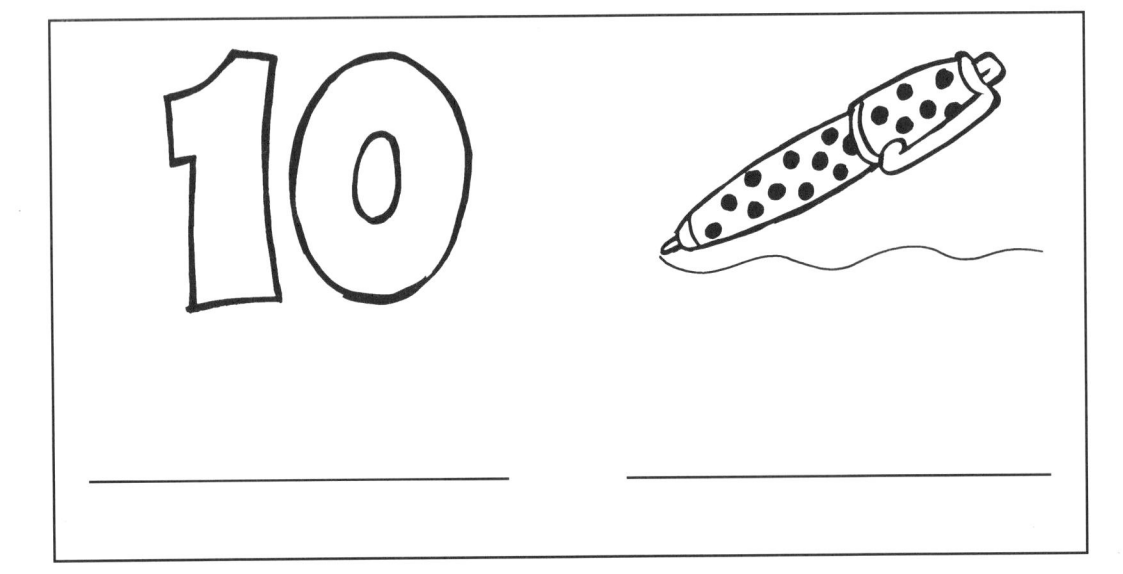

_____ _____

Focus on Literacy Starter Level Skills Pack © HarperCollinsPublishers Ltd 2001

Skills Master 98
Unit 25

Name _____

Animal noises

What noises do these animals make?

moo   cluck   oink   baa   woof

Skills Master 99
Unit 25

Name _____

sh is for sheep

Join the words to the correct pictures.

- sheep  
- shell 
- shed 
- ship
- shoes 
- shark 
- shelf

Focus on Literacy Starter Level Skills Pack © HarperCollinsPublishers Ltd 2001

Skills Master 100
Unit 25

Name

Animal names

Circle the letters that are in each animal's name.

a e
h
p n
t
P i
y g

hen

pig

Write words that rhyme.

hen

pig

t _____

b _____

m _____

d _____

p _____

w _____

Focus on Literacy Starter Level Skills Pack © HarperCollinsPublishers Ltd 2001

Skills Master 101
Unit 26

Name _____

Yummy alphabet

Write the initial letter next to each picture.

a b c d e f g h i j k l m n o p q r s t u v w x y z

Focus on Literacy Starter Level Skills Pack © HarperCollinsPublishers Ltd 2001

Skills Master 102
Unit 26

Name _____

Shopping list

Write a list of the things you would need for a picnic.

Alphabet fruits

Join each letter to its capital.

A B C D E F G H I J K L M

b a p s l o g

N O P Q R S T U V W X Y Z

Skills Master 104
Unit 26

Name _____

Alphabet maze

Find your way through the maze from **a** to **z**.

Start →

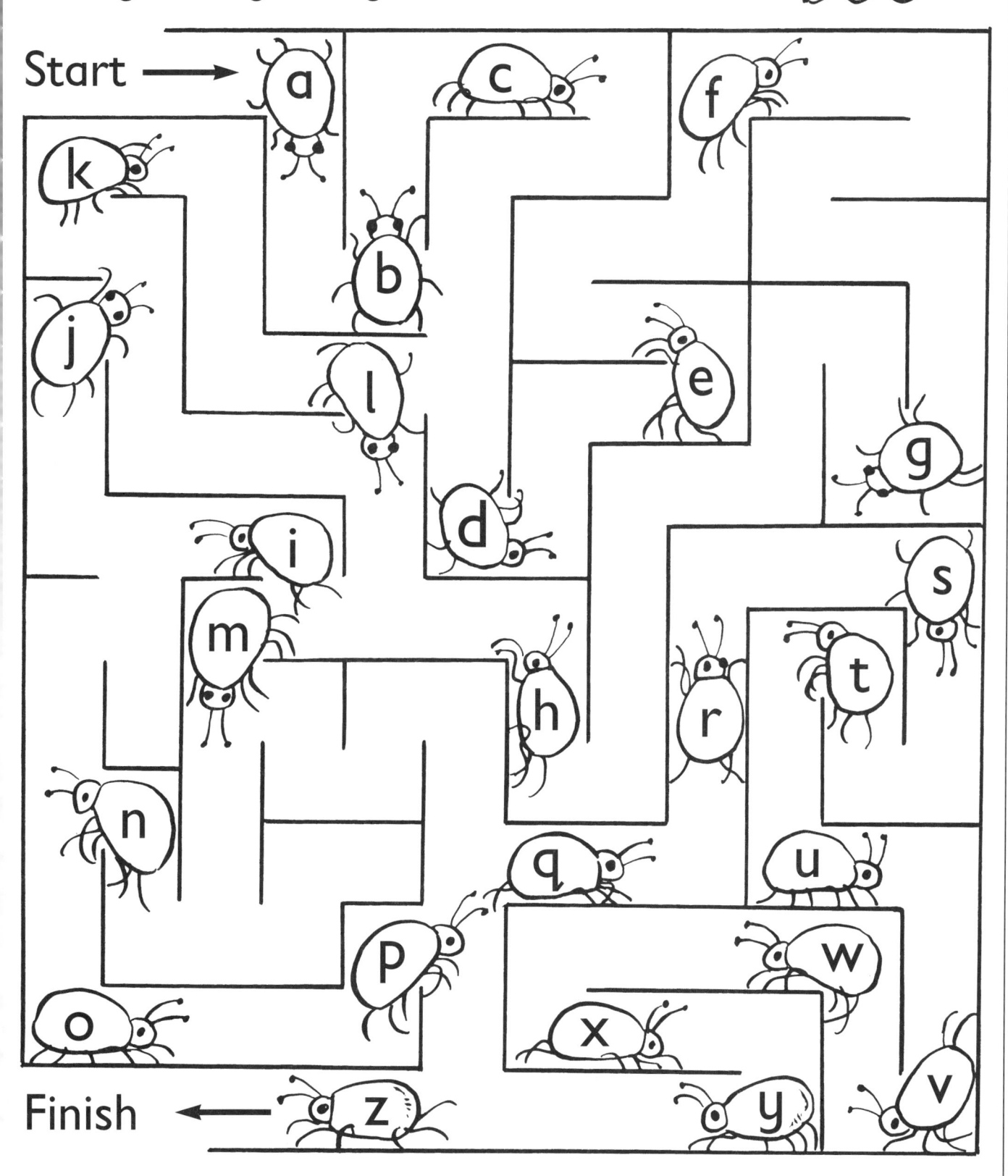

a b c d e f g h i j k l m n o p q r s t u v w x y z

Focus on Literacy Starter Level Skills Pack © HarperCollinsPublishers Ltd 2001

Skills Master 105
Unit 27

Name _____

Mm is for mice

Write the letter **m**.

m m m m m m ___ ___ ___

Write **m** in the box next to things that begin with **m**.

Nn is for newt

Write the letter **n**.

n n n n n n _____ _____ _____ _____

Write **n** in the box next to things that begin with **n**.

Opposites

Write the correct word in each space.

| sad | wet | up | hot |

dry _____

cold _____

down _____

happy _____

**Skills Master 108
Unit 27**

Name _____

Words beginning with m

Write **m** in each space to make words.

__ix   __ap   __ug

__op   __an   __ilk

Write the words under the pictures.

_____   _____   _____

_____   _____   _____

Focus on Literacy Starter Level Skills Pack © HarperCollinsPublishers Ltd 2001

Skills Master 109
Unit 28

Name _____

Words with a

Write the letter **a**.

a a a a a a ___ ___ ___ ___ ___

Label each picture.

| bag | jam | tap |

_____   _____   _____

Use the letters to make words that rhyme with **man**.

c
 f
P
 r
v

__ an

__ an

__ an

__ an

__ an

Focus on Literacy Starter Level Skills Pack © HarperCollinsPublishers Ltd 2001

Skills Master 110
Unit 28

Name _____

The Gingerbread Man

Tell the story.

1.

2.

_____
_____

3.

4.

_____
_____

Focus on Literacy Starter Level Skills Pack © HarperCollins*Publishers* Ltd 2001

Skills Master 111
Unit 28

Name _____

Ff is for fox

Write the letter **f**.

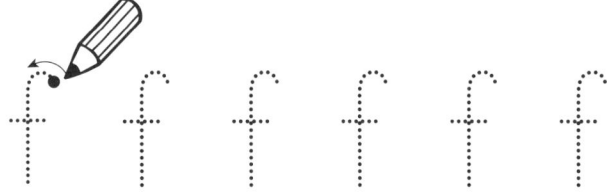

f f f f f f ___ ___ ___ ___ ___

Write **f** in the box next to things that begin with **f**.

Focus on Literacy Starter Level Skills Pack © HarperCollinsPublishers Ltd 2001

Word chain

Skills Master 112
Unit 28

Name _____

Change one letter at a time to make new words.

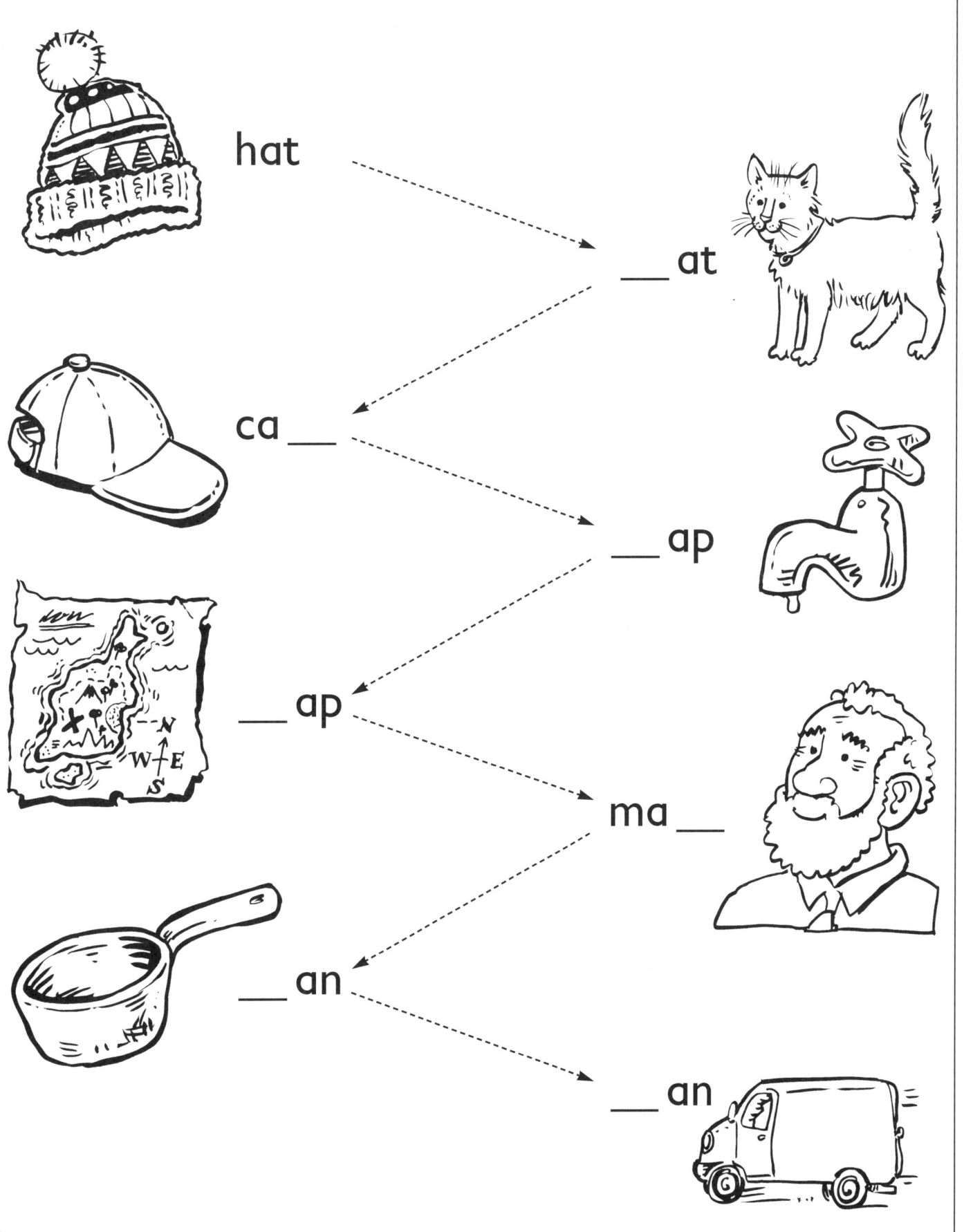

hat

__at

ca__

__ap

__ap

ma__

__an

__an

Skills Master 113
Unit 29

Name _____

Words beginning with b

Write **b** in each space to make words.

__ed __ath __us

__ag __at __all

Write the words under the pictures.

_____ _____ _____

_____ _____ _____

Focus on Literacy Starter Level Skills Pack © HarperCollinsPublishers Ltd 2001

Skills Master 114
Unit 29

Name _____

Bears

Use the words to write a sentence about each bear.

Black   like   bears   honey

_____
_____
_____ .

bamboo   Pandas   eat

_____
_____
_____ .

live   on   Polar   bears
land   icy

_____
_____
_____ .

Focus on Literacy Starter Level Skills Pack © HarperCollins*Publishers* Ltd 2001

Skills Master 115
Unit 29

Name _____

Where are the bears?

Write the correct words under each picture.

| in the bedroom | on the stairs |
| in the kitchen | in the bathroom |

_____   _____

_____   _____

_____   _____

_____   _____

Focus on Literacy Starter Level Skills Pack © HarperCollins*Publishers* Ltd 2001

Skills Master 116
Unit 29

Name _____

Busy bears

What are these bears doing?
Write each sentence next to the correct picture.

> This bear has got a fish.
> This bear is up a tree.
> This bear is sleeping.

Focus on Literacy Starter Level Skills Pack © HarperCollins*Publishers* Ltd 2001

Skills Master 117
Unit 30

Name _____

Words with i

Write the letter **i**.

i i i i i i ___ ___ ___ ___ ___

Write **i** in each space to make words.

w __ n   m __ x   d __ g

b __ n   p __ g   b __ g

Write the correct word for each picture.

_____   _____   _____

_____

Focus on Literacy Starter Level Skills Pack © HarperCollinsPublishers Ltd 2001

Skills Master 118
Unit 30

Name _____

Teddy bears' picnic

Finish the invitation.

Dear Teddy
Please come to our picnic

on _____

at _____.

There will be lots of food
and games to play.

Love from

_____

Focus on Literacy Starter Level Skills Pack © HarperCollinsPublishers Ltd 2001

Skills Master 119
Unit 30

Name _____

Words with sh

In each space, write a word with **sh** that rhymes with the first word.

bed

_____

mop

_____

dish

_____

bell

_____

Focus on Literacy Starter Level Skills Pack © HarperCollinsPublishers Ltd 2001

Skills Master 120
Unit 30

Name _____

Where is Ted?

Choose the correct word to finish each sentence.

bin   shed   bed   pig

Ted is on the
_____.

Ted is by the
_____.

Ted is with the
_____.

Ted is in the
_____.

Focus on Literacy Starter Level Skills Pack © HarperCollinsPublishers Ltd 2001

Skills Master 121

High frequency words 1

a	at	come
all	away	dad
am	big	day
and	can	dog
are	cat	for

Focus on Literacy Starter Level Skills Pack © HarperCollins*Publishers* Ltd 2001

High frequency words 2

get	in	me
go	is	mum
going	it	my
he	like	no
I	look	of

Skills Master 123

High frequency words 3

on	the	was
play	they	we
said	this	went
see	to	yes
she	up	you

Skills Master 124

Word wheel

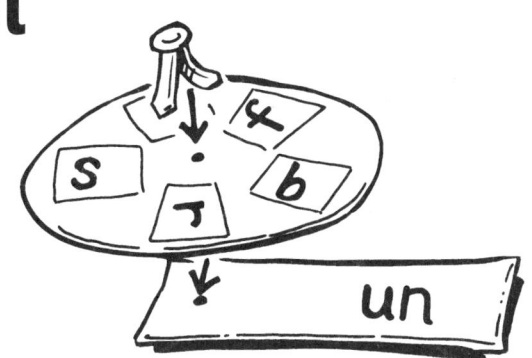

Cut out the wheel and a strip. Attach the strip under the wheel with a paper fastener. Write onsets on the wheel and a rime on the strip.

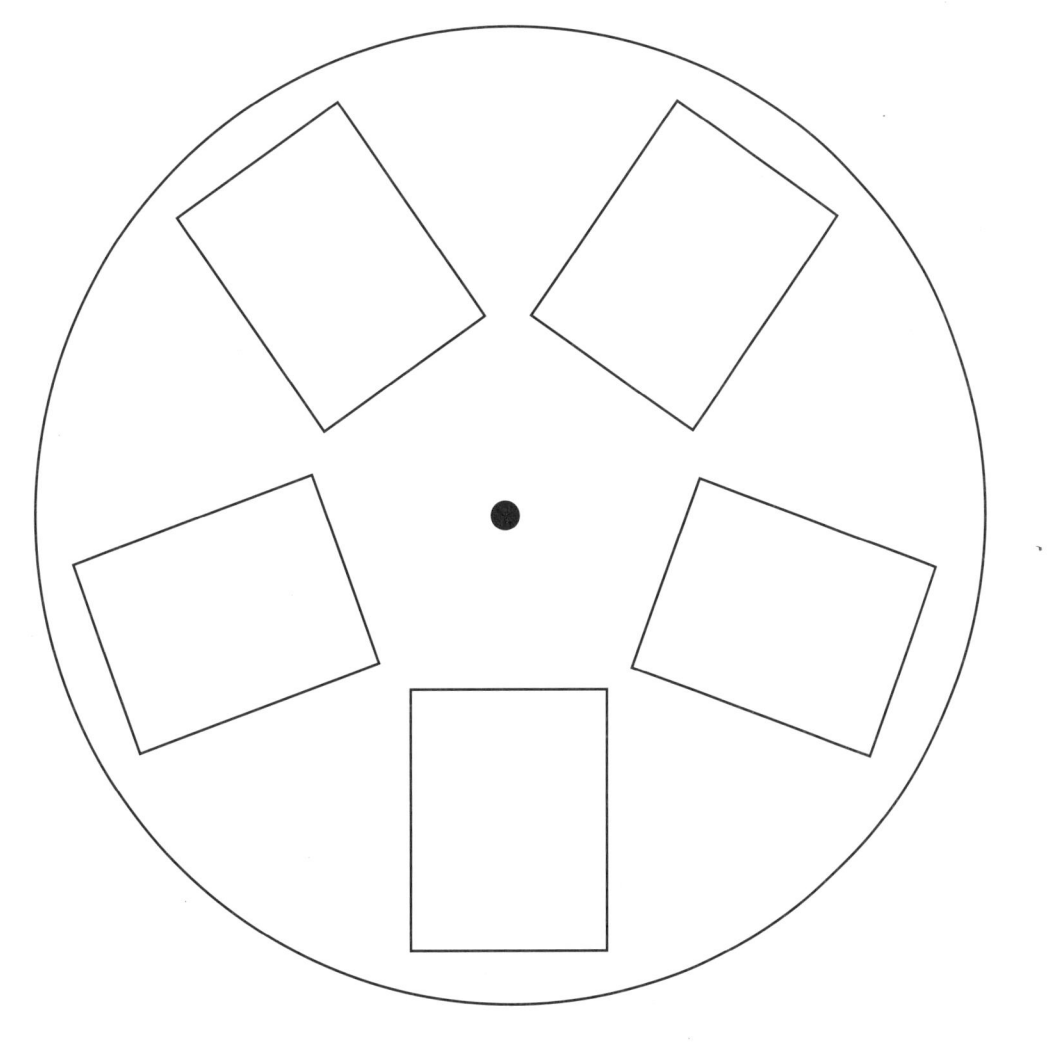

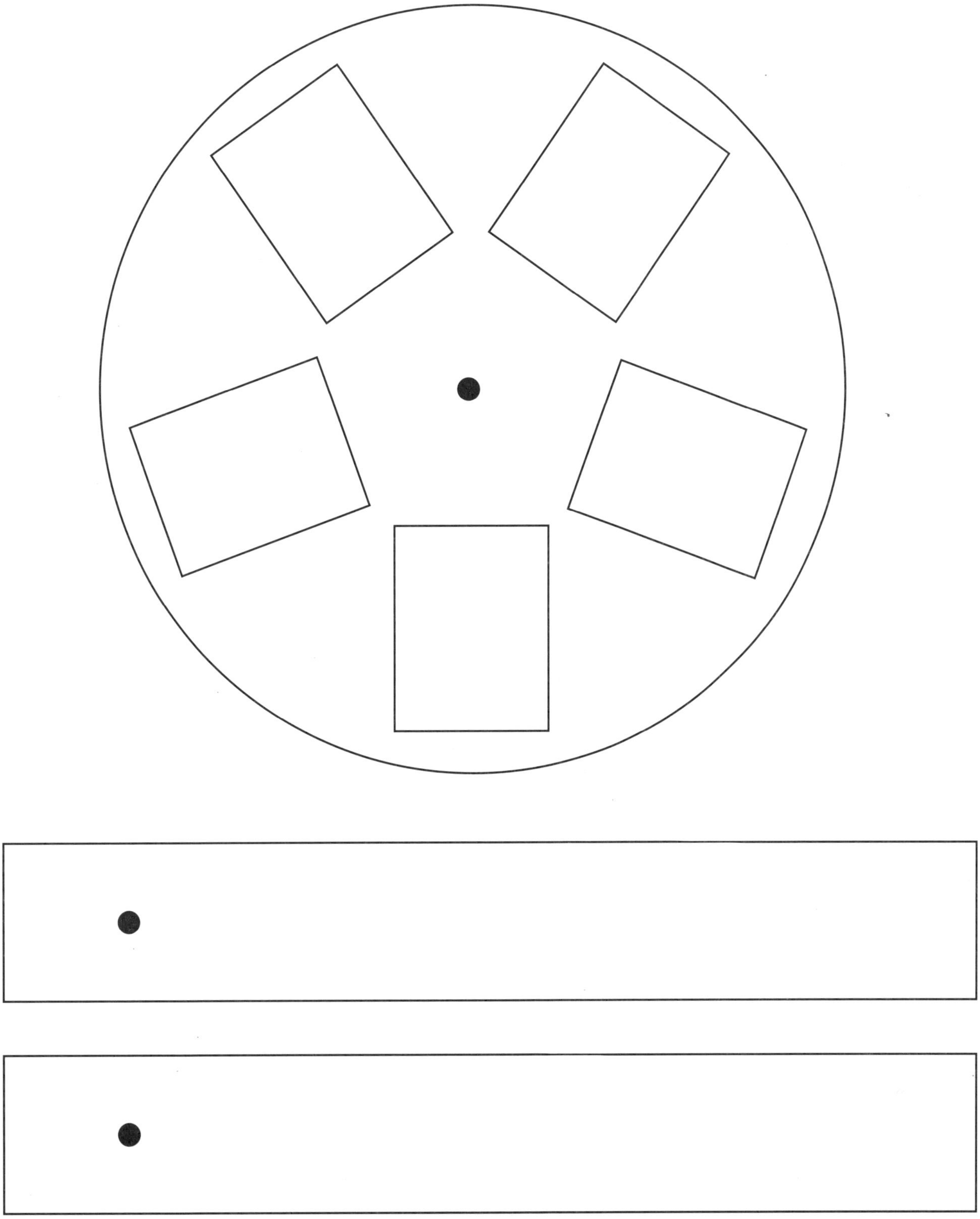

Focus on Literacy Starter Level Skills Pack © HarperCollins*Publishers* Ltd 2001

Word slide

Cut out the word frame and a strip.
Cut two slits in the frame.
Write a rime on the word frame and onsets on the strip.
Slide the strip under the slits in the frame so that the onsets appear one at a time in the space.

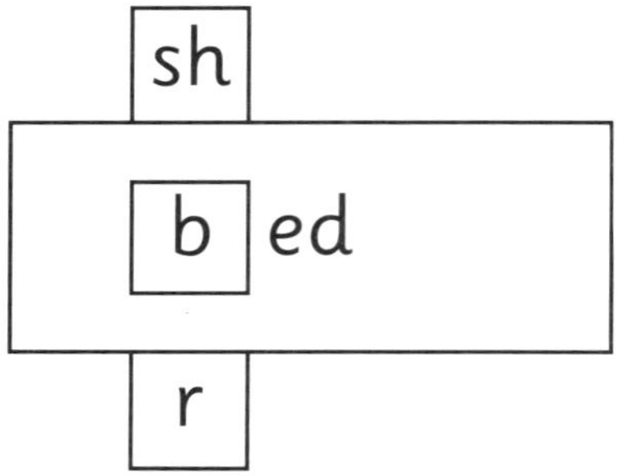

sh

b ed

r

Skills Master 125

Focus on Literacy Starter Level Skills Pack © HarperCollins*Publishers* Ltd 2001

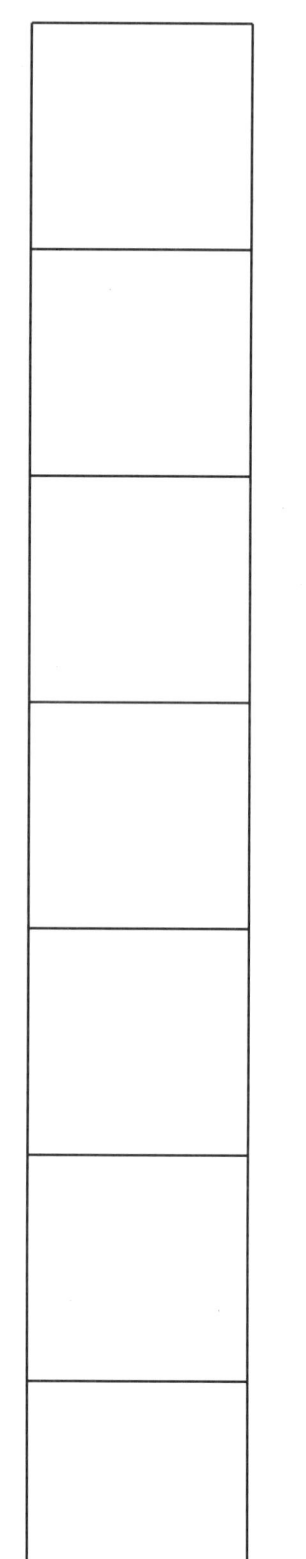